ALL RIGH
Original W

MW01001777

MERMAID HOUR
© David Valdes
Trade Edition, 2022
ISBN 978-1-63092-135-4

JUNE IS THE FIRST FALL by Yilong Liu

Synopsis: What compels people to cross mountains and seas to another country, another continent, and another culture to find their true selves? What are the journeys we take to find home and belonging? In JUNE IS THE FIRST FALL, Don, a gay Chinese man, returns home to Hawaii to rediscover missing memories of himself and his family that he moved away from. His week-long stay opens wounds with his father and sister that never healed, aggravating Don's struggle to find love and belonging in his life.

Cast Size: 3 Males, 2 Females

Mermaid Hour

by David Valdes

Mermaid Hour received a National New Play Network Rolling World Premiere at Borderlands Theater (Tucson, Arizona), Milagro Theater (Portland, Oregon), Mixed Blood Theater (Minneapolis, Minnesota)*, and Actor's Theater of Charlotte (Charlotte, North Carolina), from March to May 2018, featuring the following creative teams, listed in order of rolling production.

PILAR: Alida Holguin Gunn, Nelda Reyes, Thallis Santesteban, Adyana La Torre
BIRD: Sean William Dupont, Jed Arkley, Michael Hanna, Jeremy DeCarlos
VI: Jay Garcia, Jaryn Lasentia, Azoralla Arroyo Caballero, Toni Reali
JACOB: Eddie Diaz, Kai Hynes, Meng Xiong, Alec Celis
MIKA: Kat McIntosh, Barbie Wu, Sheena Jason, Amy Wada
MERPERSON/CRUX: Eddie Diaz, Michael Cavazos, Cat Hammond, Alex Aguilar

Directed by Glen Coffman, Sacha Reich, Leah Anderson, and Laley Lippard

*Featuring music by Eric Mayson

Setting:

The 2010s. A working class liberal-ish town in Massachusetts, well away from Boston.

A few items might suggest the Bardisa-Nickerson home, all elements should be easily moved or repurposed. There should be some anchors to locate the house but there should be ample open, transformational space onstage. It's not a kitchen sink drama. Their world, their child, their lives, are always on the edge of change.

Cast:

VIOLET BARDISA-NICKERSON, a girl assigned male at birth, 12 going on 15, mixed ethnicity.
BIRD NICKERSON, 30s, her dad, any race, working class with two jobs.
PILAR BARDISA, 30s, her mom, Cuban-American, nurse's aid on the way to being a nurse.
JACOB ENDO, Vi's crush, 12, Japanese-American.
MIKA ENDO, 40s, Jacob's mother, Japanese-American.
CRUX DUMAY/MERPERSON, 30s, genderqueer, not the same race as Bird.

The play is written for six actors. You may not undouble Crux/Merperson.

Race is not firmly prescribed for any of the roles, but the indications above are what I envision. Pilar should be played by a Latinx actor; the Endos should be played by Asian actors (you may change the family name and grandparents' city to match their origin if desired). The play may not be staged with an all-Caucasian cast without explicit written consent.

On casting VI: If you are not able to cast an actress that young, a high school student or very youthful college-aged student can work. Vi must be played by trans or genderqueer actor AMAB and the casting should not be taken lightly; preference is for a trans female actor, followed by a gender-nonconforming actor. Note: You may not cast a cisgender female actor, period, or a cisgender male actor who does not self-identify as gender queer or nonbinary.

CRUX must be play by an actor who is gender nonconforming (nonbinary, genderqueer, or trans); note that CRUX is not a drag queen.

Pronunciation notes:

Pilar is pronounced Pee-LAR (with the R rolled.)
"Mija" is run together as one word, pronounced mee-ha, Spanish for "my daughter."
Mika is pronounced mee-ka.

MERMAID HOUR

SCENE ONE:

(The mid-2010s. A working-class liberal town nearish Boston. The home of the Bardisa-Nickersons.)

(BIRD comes into the living room with a six-pack of soda, followed by VI with plates and a blanket. They set up a picnic for 3 on the floor, VI's plate in the middle.)

VI: And THEN he told me about rainbow parties.

BIRD: Am I gonna want to know what a rainbow party is?

VI: *(Ah ha.)* You don't know? Ha! I bet Celia five bucks.

BIRD: You bet real money? That's stupid, honey.

VI: It's not stupid. I won $5.

BIRD: *(Looks at set up.)* You forgot chopsticks.

VI: You get em.

BIRD: Setting the table's your job.

VI: *(Think she's clever.)* Yeah, but this is the floor.

BIRD: *(Oh yeah?)* We can eat at the table if you like.

VI: *(One more try.)* Thursday's TV picnic!

BIRD: Then don't be an asshole about table versus floor.

VI: *(Beat)* Fine. *(Not too grudging. They kinda love giving each other shit.)*

BIRD: *(To himself.)* Probably coulda skipped asshole. *(Whistles as he finishes set up.)*

VI: *(Back in with the chopsticks.)* So…

BIRD: Rainbow parties?

VI: Rainbow parties are when the same number of girls and boys go to a party and all the girls wear different color lipsticks and then, you know…

BIRD: I don't know.

VI: *(Makes an O shape with her mouth.)* And the winner is the boy with the most colors on his…

BIRD: Hold up.

VI: …on his, you know. *(She mimes something going into a girl's mouth.)*

BIRD: You are seriously telling me this?

VI: You always say we can talk about anything!

BIRD: No, Mami says that, I just try to play along.

(PILAR enters in Nurse's Aide uniform, looking pooped, overloaded by carrying a shoulder bag, some groceries, and a bag of take-out boxes of Chinese food, which she hands off.)

VI: Fine, I'll ask Mami.

PILAR: Ask Mami in a minute.

(She exits with the grocery bag.)

BIRD: Now it's a question? A moment ago you were just telling me and it was bad enough.

VI: So...Does it count as sex?

BIRD: Of course it counts!

PILAR: *(Enters.)* Does what count?

VI: When a girl puts her lips on a guy's—

PILAR: *(Shoots BIRD a look.)* When what?

VI: *(Finally a little embarrassed but forging on.)* Not to... *(Can't say it.)* you know...Just to leave her color on it before the next girl.

PILAR: My god mija—why are you asking about rainbow parties?

BIRD: *(To PILAR.)* How do you know rainbow parties?

PILAR: *(To Bird, dismissive.)* Oprah. And parenting boards. *(To VI, serious.)* You know it's an urban legend, right?

VI: Celia said—

PILAR: Even if it was real, in what universe is it not sexual for girls to put a bunch of penises in their mouths?

VI: You don't have to say it like that!

PILAR: You brought it up.

VI: *(Trying to move forward.)* Celia says it counts because the girl's mouth isn't a virgin anymore but Jacob says it doesn't really count cause it's really quick and no one's really doing anything.

BIRD: Guess which one of those two still gets to come over?

PILAR: *(Supremely unruffled. She knows what she's doing.)* Beyond the fact that putting a penis in your mouth is like putting your mouth on a lollipop covered with potential viruses—*(VI recoils.)*

BIRD: Jeez, honey.

PILAR: Adolescent boys are famous for their terrible hygiene, which means you might be getting globs of old—

VI: *(What hell has she unleased here?)* STOP!

PILAR: Ok, ok. But you know this makes the girls toys for the boys while the boys get the big thrill.

BIRD: And we know you're all about girl power these days.

VI: "These days"?

PILAR: So the question isn't "Does it count as sex?" but "Is it risky and demeaning?" Tell that to Celia and Jacob. *(Adopting her sage progressive mom voice.)* Sexual desire can be a wonderful thing when you're ready—*(VI would love her to shut up.)*— but mija, I mean it: watch where you put your lips.

BIRD: —and your penis.

VI: DAD!

PILAR: Bird!

BIRD: I'm just saying. Either end of this stick, I don't want you on it. You're friggin' 12 and you shouldn't even be hearing about this shit, much less arguing the fine points.

VI: You guys freak out about every little thing I bring up!

PILAR: You never bring up anything little.

BIRD: It's true. Tell me you cheated on a test, I beg you.

VI: NOW you're ganging up on me!

PILAR: *(Trying to steer things light.)* We're parents— that's our job.

BIRD: And we're good at it, right?

11

VI: *(Knows how to get them.)* Yeah, fine. You can have a kid who doesn't tell you about rainbow parties, you know. *(She gets up.)* The scallion pancakes are mine. *(Grabs them. Storms off.)*

BIRD: "Rainbow parties?"

PILAR: *(Mad.)* "Penis?"

BIRD: Well, she has one. I just wanna be clear: no rainbow nothing.

PILAR: But now you've made her regret telling us.

BIRD: I'm thinking your "penises dipped in horror" didn't help.

PILAR: *(Ignores that.)* Doctor Eggleston says she has to feel comfortable talking to us.

BIRD: Doctor Eggleston says a lot of things. *(A glare from Pilar. Looks through the boxes.)* They forgot the General Gau.

PILAR: *(Looks.)* And sent two cashew chicken. *(Groans. They love General Gau.)* Nothing can be easy.

BIRD: Do we still let her go to the Halloween Party?

PILAR: Why wouldn't we?

BIRD: How do we know it's not one of these rainbow jobs?

PILAR: It's all talk, Bird.

BIRD: *(Thinking about himself at 12.)* I wasn't. All talk. *(Looks off.)* Do we start without her?

PILAR: It's *Project Runway*. She'll never forgive us if we do. *(They do a rock, paper, scissors. He loses, sighs, rises.)*

BIRD: If I don't come out in 10 minutes, I will you my crab Rangoon.

(Bird exits. Dark on living room.)

(Lights up on VI and JACOB imagined in their rooms. Both are on their phones. Their bodies should be positioned like they are facing each other and interacting with each other, but their eyes stay on their phones. Jacob is slender and lanky; a noodle of a cool kid, almost a year older than VI but in the same class, he reads queer.)

VI: Is Nguyen going to be there?

JACOB: Why? Do you like him?

VI: No! He smells like Axe!

JACOB: He's gay anyway.

VI: Huh?

JACOB: He so wanted to kiss me but I told him to grow up first.

VI: Duh. You're the same age.

13

JACOB: 12 is a massive year. Like, my 12 is to his 12 like 20 is to 15.

VI: What kind of 12 am I?

JACOB: You're a special case. *(Tiniest beat.)* Nguyen's not coming. His mom doesn't like my mom.

VI: I wish I had your mom. She's so…*(Pulling out high praise.)* sophisticated.

JACOB: *(Eyeroll.)* What. Ever. *(Shrug.)* Your parents are cool. Well, your mom is. Did you ask about the shots again?

VI: Daddy freaks out, like breaks into a sweat. I'm trying to wait till we see Dr. Eggleston.

JACOB: That's a terrible name.

VI: She's nice!

JACOB: Could be worse; she could be Spermelston.

VI: You make fun of everything.

JACOB: So do you! You said Ms. Gupta's unibrow looks like someone underlined her forehead.

VI: She's the only one who gets me.

JACOB: I get you.

VI: Only grown-up. Around here. I wish I lived in New York. *(She says this like it's the promised land, but JACOB just snorts.)* What?

JACOB: Don't get mad but…

VI: *(Immediately upset.)* You think I'm not cool enough?

JACOB: Cool for this place, maybe, but…*(A shrug.)* I don't think you could handle it.

VI: You did!

JACOB: Um, yeah, but I was raised there—I knew the subway by third grade. You can't find your way to fifth period.

VI: That only happened once! *(A look from JACOB.)* Twice—but that was weeks ago!

JACOB: Face it. You're a small-town girl.

VI: Take that back!

JACOB: *(Doesn't. Grins and moves on.)* I heard it may snow this weekend.

VI: It'll kill my costume. I'll have to wear a hoodie or—

JACOB: We're not, like, trick or treating. It's all inside.

VI: I just wanted to look pretty the whole time.

JACOB: *(Casual.)* You always look pretty.

VI: *(Hopeful.)* I do?

JACOB: Duh. You're like, beautiful.

VI: Awwww…

JACOB: *(Eye roll.)* You're such a girl.

VI: Right?

(BIRD steps into the room, pissed.)

BIRD: Are you on the phone?

VI: No.

(VI hangs up and JACOB is plunged into darkness immediately.)

BIRD: Give me that. *(She does.)* What are the rules, Vi?

VI: He called me!

BIRD: I didn't ask. What are the rules?

VI: Phones only in public space. Mami says she only lets you have that rule so you feel better.

BIRD: Lemme guess. "He" is Jacob. Well, he helped you lose the phone for a day. Who feels what now?

VI: Daddy! The party's tomorrow night—I have to be able to text.

BIRD: You have a costume and your ride's all set—I don't think you do.

VI: *(Pulling a PILAR.)* We need a family meeting to talk about the phone rules. I'm 12 and this is getting a little old.

BIRD: You're not gonna get old if you keep this up. Phone is mine until the party. And if you complain—we can talk about the party, too.

VI: *(She knows she's lost this one.)* Daddyyyyy.

BIRD: *(Knows that she knows. Redirects.)* Project *Runway*'s on. *(She wants to watch but doesn't want to relent.)* It's the Unconventional Materials challenge. *(He takes a step toward the door and then steps back.)* Don't be too pissed.

VI: *(Doesn't want to give in. Decides not to.)* I'm not. I'm tired

BIRD: *(Not sure how to read that.)* Ok…

VI: *(Big show of fake sleepiness; it's meant to look fake and he's meant to know she means it to. Yawns, yawns dramatically, stretches.)* I need my beauty sleep.

BIRD: Oh. Alright then. *(He kisses the top of her head but she pulls away.)* Alright.

(Lights down there and back up in living room.)

(PILAR is on her laptop, googling, like always. She leans in with interest. Shakes her head, or nods maybe, at whatever she sees. Pauses when BIRD crosses back in.)

PILAR: No?

BIRD: *(Mimics VI.)* "I need my beauty sleep."

PILAR: I bet she thinks this is making you pay.

BIRD: It kind of is. Thursdays are fun. *(Shrugs.)* Is your laptop coming to TV Picnic?

PILAR: You weren't here, so I—

BIRD: I know.

PILAR: I was checking out the new links from Eggleston.

BIRD: She gets to come to TV Picnic too?

PILAR: *(A dig.)* One of us has to read up on this.

BIRD: And look at that: one of us is. All the time. *(Beat.)* D'you ask Eggleston my question?

PILAR: It was embarrassing.

BIRD: Bet she's heard worse. So?

PILAR: Yes, I did, and, like I said: children this sure never go back.

BIRD: Never or hardly ever?

PILAR: She sent me a link. There were studies in Holland.

BIRD: You learned Dutch!

PILAR: If you'd even glance at the internet, you could learn a thing or two.

BIRD: Does porn count?

PILAR: *(Holds up her tablet.)* Any time you want, I've bookmarked all the links.

BIRD: And they all say it's safe?

PILAR: *(Clicks on one.)* This girl started puberty blockers at exactly Vi's age. And she went to the same guy at Children's Hospital that Eggleston likes.

BIRD: *(Pressing ahead.)* They all say it's safe?

PILAR: And look at her!

BIRD: They don't. Or you'd answer me.

PILAR: Ay querrido, you're just trying to look ignorant.

BIRD: Because I don't trust the internet? Last year, you were sure you had ALS because your arm was tired.

PILAR: Tired and weak, and a little, I don't know, something.

BIRD: Because you googled the early warning signs, which are also the same warning signs that you had just worked a double at the nursing home.

PILAR: Just look at her, ok? *(He takes the tablet.)* Isn't she pretty?

BIRD: *(Looks but then gets distracted by what he sees.)* Wait—is this the cost? *(Holds it toward her, then looks again.)* MONTHLY?

PILAR: Health care is expensive.

BIRD: Will insurance cover this?

PILAR: *(Shrugs.)* Some or all. I'm figuring it out.

BIRD: Your plan has a huge deductible. Kill me now.

PILAR: At least my job offers health insurance.

BIRD: Ok, after we shell out two thousand bucks so Vi can look pretty in a dress, will your plan cover the other ten months? Or do I need a third lousy job?

PILAR: Really, this is about the money?

BIRD: We're adults. Who live in America. Everything is about the money. *(Softer.)* Peel, think about this. We have no savings. We skipped summer vacation because my shifts got cut to half. She's taking guitar instead of violin cause it's the instrument we have lying around.

PILAR: I'm working as much as I can.

BIRD: That's not the point.

PILAR: What is?

BIRD: The point—*(Stops.)*

PILAR: Go ahead.

BIRD: The money, the safety, the friggin' everything. It's clicking on a picture of a kid who was once someone's little boy and saying how pretty she looks and wondering, does he still have his junk? Or did they cut it off? It's living in a world where I'm thinking, did they cut it off? It's cutting it off.

PILAR: *(Trying to solve this.)* Querrido, it's just shots to buy us time.

BIRD: *(Not relenting.)* Until they cut it off.

PILAR: *(Now she's over it.)* Do you hear yourself? *(He shrugs.)* Someday, she's going to grow up and fall in love and get married--

BIRD: Not if she's smart.

PILAR: *(Blowing by that.)*— and when you walk her down the aisle and she is happy in who she is, none of that is going matter. *(He is simmering and doesn't reply. She thinks maybe she's got him. She gets up, starts packing up the Chinese.)* We're lucky to live in a time where we can look this up ourselves. Imagine how hard it used to be! *(Exits.)*

BIRD: *(To himself, looking at the last page left open.)* Yeah, cause it's SO easy now. *(Lights down.)*

(VI's room, a little later. She is staring into the dark until a patch of light illuminates the MERPERSON. Their appearance should be majestic, beautiful, eerie, and even a little unsettling all at once. They should have something approximating a fantastic tail. They are not a garden-variety mermaid, not easily gendered or sexualized; they are beautiful in a way that doesn't conform to norms, but instead capitalizes most on the graces of the performer. They radiate with self-confidence and warmth.)

21

(At this point, the audience should have no idea from where this vision comes. The language is poetic and the MERPERSON means every word.)

MERPERSON: *(Out.)* Arise, my loves.

You are the children of beauty and light, the gift of the heavens that cover both the land and the sea.

Never kneel before the earth, never waste your tears on ground that does not welcome you.

Arise and be all that you are, all that I am.

I was a girl a long time ago. I was a boy a long time ago. I was a mortal a long time ago.

I am not mortal!
I am not land or sea! I am heavens.

The secret of our kind is that we are not in between, but above.

See how I shine!
(A brilliant light effect should dazzle us for a moment.)
See how I glow in the Mermaid Hour!
Glow, my children! Glow!

(Lights out on the MERPERSON.)

End scene.

SCENE TWO:

(Halloween. Lights up on VIOLET wearing a long green mermaid tail topped with a big fuzzy purple hoodie to ward off the cold. Her hair is hidden beneath a red wig that tumbles past her shoulders and she has a starfish hair clip. At her feet we see a sparkly shoulder bag.)

(PILAR is kneeling, working on the costume, hand- sewing on the last sequins as fast as she can. She looks frazzled. VI's phone is next to the sewing kit.)

VI: They'll be here in like seconds!

PILAR: I'm trying sweetheart.

VI: It's going to look unfinished.

PILAR: Mija, it's a needle and thread and sequins: you could have done it yourself.

VI: You hate it when I get in your sewing kit.

PILAR: *(True enough.)* I do. *(VIOLET turns a little as if looking in a mirror.)* Honey—you cannot move and expect me to finish this.

VI: *(Touching the wig, which is a little voluminous and curly.)* Does this look hoochy?

PILAR: "Hoochy?" *(It kind of does.)* You begged for it long enough.

VI: I want better hair.

PILAR: Everyone does. *(Time to lie a little.)* It's pretty.

VI: If we lived in New York City, you could get good wigs at like the drug store.

PILAR: Yeah? Who says?

VI: Jacob. He says drag queens used to buy all their stuff at the pharmacy on his block. *(With utter disdain.)* It's not like here.

PILAR: How do we stand it? *(Pulling a stitch through.)*

VI: Right? It was boring before Jacob.

PILAR: What's he going as?

VI: The Wolf.

PILAR: There's a wolf in Little Mermaid?

VI: Duh. It's not a theme party. He's THE wolf, like Big Bad.

PILAR: What about Celia? And STOP MOVING!

VI: She was going to be Little Red Riding Hood but her mom said not if Jacob was a wolf. Isn't that stupid?

PILAR: *(Doesn't answer. Sits back.)* Done. Thank god.

VI: *(Spinning the conversation away and spinning her tail. Thrilled.)* Awww, it shines!

PILAR: It ought to, I herniated a disc for it.

VI: You're the best. THE best.

PILAR: Can I get that in writing? *(Looks at watch.)* Let's get some pictures before you go.

VI: *(Hops down.)* I'm good.

PILAR: I'll be quick.

VI: Probably should wait for them out front anyway.

PILAR: I did all that work, you really think it's not going on Facebook?

VI: Celia's dad has the good camera.

PILAR: Mija, I'm not asking for a kidney here. Come on. *(Goes to unzip the hoodie.)*

VI: You can't just do that, I'm 12!

PILAR: *(Gets it)* Ok. *(Steps back.)* You do it. Right now. *(A stand-off.)*

VI: I'm not a baby.

PILAR: Open it.

(VI stands with her back facing us. Only PILAR can see the front of the hoodie.)

VI: *(Unzips partway. In self-defense.)* Celia's costume has a mini-skirt and fishnets.

PILAR: *(Sees the front view we can't.)* OH MY GOD.

(VI unzips, so hoodie is fully open toward her mom.)

VI: *(Defiant)* I'm a MERMAID.

PILAR: A clam shell bra. Really? You think there's any chance of me letting you leave here in a bra and nothing else?

VI: And a tail! Bra and a tail! It's what she wears, Mami!

PILAR: I say yes to a lot of things but I'm not letting a 12 -year-old leave here in a bra.

VI: *(Reaching up under the hoodie from behind, unclasps the clam bra, which she drops. PILAR now has a view of a bare chest. VI is defiant.)* How about this? That better?

(We hear a car horn.)

PILAR: Where's the top I made?

VI: In my bag. But it's not what she wears!

PILAR: I can call Celia's dad: "Hi, sorry you're in the driveway but we've had a change of plans."

VI: You're such a prude!

PILAR: "Prude"? Did you get that from a vocab test?

(VI scoops up her bag and stomps off.)

VI: I hate you.

(We hear a ding. VI's phone gets a text. PILAR reads it.)

PILAR: "We're here. No rush obvi." Right, the honking and the text are just for fun.

VI: *(Back in view in the top PILAR made.)* Clams on top at least? *(PILAR hesitates.)* Please? Please.

(PILAR knows that this can be a win. She helps VI put the clams on over the shirt. They're both happier and PILAR uses the moment to snap a really sweet selfie of them together. VI breaks the pose first, grabs her bag and hoodie, and starts to head off.)

PILAR: Here's your phone. *(Hands it to her.)* Call me if you need anything.

VI: You mean call you if anything goes horribly horribly wrong.

PILAR: Your words, kiddo.

VI: *(Kisses PILAR. Helpful.)* You know, some of my friends' moms…take pills for anxiety.

PILAR: *(PILAR scoops the discarded hoodie up off the floor.)* Some have housekeepers too.

VI: *(Inspiration for a joke.)* Wait: who picks up the mess at King Triton's?

PILAR: Who does what? *(Gets it.)* The mer-Maid. Good one.

VI: I know, right? *(Exits.)*

(Lights up across the stage on the kitchen bar, where BIRD is prepping a salad. He has an open beer, nearly finished, and a closed beer. A glass of wine and bottle wait for PILAR. There are Whole Foods bags on the counter. PILAR crosses to him, the lights going out where she'd been.)

BIRD: She's off, yeah?

PILAR: Ay, Celia's dad and the honking! The man never learned manners.

BIRD: *(Nods at the bag.)* Get lost on your way home tonight?

PILAR: I knew you'd say that

BIRD: Star Market's just up the street.

PILAR: *(She takes out some items that remain in the bag—plantains, blueberries, two heads of cauliflower.)* You can't just buy vegetables anywhere. *(She pulls out a small cake in a pretty box.)*

BIRD: Yeah? Is cake a vegetable?

PILAR: You really want a Star Market cake?

BIRD: At Star Market prices, sure. Unless we became the 1 % and you didn't tell me.

PILAR: It's *date night.*

BIRD: You bring me to all the nicest places. *(He finishes the salad, sets down the knife.)*

PILAR: We have three or four hours with no Vi and we don't even have to pay a sitter. We deserve cake that doesn't taste like Star Market. *(She takes cutting board.)* What's making you so grumpy?

BIRD: Supplier at work is being a dick. My daughter has a crush on a boy who knows about rainbow parties. *(Nods at the cutting board where she has set cauliflower.)* Cauliflower on date night.

PILAR: I know, I know. But it was on sale at Whole Foods and I saw it and thought—

BIRD: "Bird hates Cauliflower"?

PILAR: No—"When was the last time we had cauliflower?" And you don't hate it, not globally. You like it when I bake it all covered in cheese and breadcrumbs.

BIRD: I'll eat anything covered in cheese and breadcrumbs.

PILAR: I just haven't cooked that sort of thing lately because of all the fat and empty calories. Why do that to myself when I'm trying to eat right? And I really am, not that you can tell.

BIRD: I can.

PILAR: Really?

BIRD: The cake is small. And the cauliflower is huge.

PILAR: *(Deflated)* Oh.

BIRD: I was kidding. *(Thinks this will help prove he noticed.)* Your blue sweater's less tight now—

PILAR: *(!?!)* What?

BIRD: *(Unwisely finishing the thought in his head.)*— though I don't see how cake helps.

PILAR: *(Furiously splits the cauliflower. Muttering.)* "All things in moderation," Bird, that's what they say. *(Not looking at him.)* Maybe apply that theory to opening your mouth.

BIRD: Whoa. Who's grumpy now?

PILAR: *(Waves the knife.)* I'm not grumpy, I'm tense. The stuff with the shots—

BIRD: Here we go.

PILAR: I can't say how I'm feeling?

BIRD: Welcome to my world.

PILAR: You're kidding me.

BIRD: I got like one minute to say how I was and then you were busy defending your crap taste in vegetables.

PILAR: You started it.

BIRD: You set me up—I hate cauliflower.

PILAR: Oh my god, querrido, you're on to me! I do, I go to Whole Foods just looking for things to piss you off.

BIRD: Good to have a skill.

(He drinks. She chops cauliflower until it's useless Sweeps the florets into the trash. Between peace offering and guilt trip.)

PILAR: We can order take out.

BIRD: You still want to eat with me?

PILAR: Despite you being a lousy date? *(He shrugs. She shrugs. This is a yes.)*

BIRD: *(Pulls out phone.)* Kebab House? Golden Raj?

PILAR: You choose. I'm having cake.

BIRD: I'll go pick it up. No need to pay extra.

PILAR: Sure. *(Doesn't look at him.)*

BIRD: Night doesn't have to be lost.

(She manages a tight smile but leaves it there. He hesitates and then exits. She stares at the cake.)

End scene.

SCENE THREE:

(Across the stage, lights up on VI and JACOB in heated discussion. VI has been crying.)

VI: But your mom said she was cool with me!

JACOB: She is. Usually.

VI: Make her stop Jacob—please!

JACOB: I can't make her do anything.

VI: They're going to flip out.

JACOB: She's already on the phone.

VI: She told me I was beautiful when I got here.

JACOB: What does that have to do with it?

VI: But she really just thinks I'm a freak!

JACOB: Vi, she saw.

VI: *(Stubborn.)* We didn't do anything. You were just showing me!.

JACOB: *(Can't believe she's being so dense.)* Um, yeah, my junk.

VI: Doesn't she know anything? *(Too loud.)* My doctor says sex play is normal.

JACOB: Don't call it sex!

VI: You're yelling at me!

JACOB: Oh my God, Vi, I wish you'd stayed home!

VI: I hate you.

JACOB: *(Crestfallen.)* I didn't mean it. *(He waits. Waits.)* Now say you didn't. *(Beat. VI is silent.)* Come on, Vi.

VI: If I was a boy, just gay, would you like me better?

JACOB: That's stupid.

VI: It's not stupid. *(Beat.)* I don't hate you.

JACOB: *(Grinning.)* Yeah. I figured. *(Then quieter.)* Your doctor really said to do stuff with your friends?

VI: Well....

JACOB: *(Dammit! He'd really hoped it was true.)* Oh.

VI: I read it online. But I'm pretty sure it's *so* normal.

(We hear a car door slam and the beep of a lock. The kids both react and then head off away from the sound, miserable.)

(To one side of the stage, not too close to the kids, we see an elegant woman, Jacob's mother MIKA, dressed in expensive casual wear. If she hadn't sworn off smoking after her time abroad, she'd be smoking now.)

MIKA: Hi guys. *(She smiles nervously at them.)* The kids are in the TV room. I thought we should—

PILAR: Have some privacy. Of course!

MIKA: Do you want anything to drink?

BIRD: PILAR:
I do.   No—I'm fine.

MIKA: I'm with Bird on this. *(To BIRD.)* Red? White?

BIRD: Beer?

MIKA: *(A beer drinker she is not; but a host she is.)* Oh. I may have some left from Labor Day. *(Exits.)*

PILAR: You couldn't wait?

BIRD: Neither could she. I'm guessing we're going to need it.

(MIKA comes back with a red for herself and beer for BIRD.)

MIKA: *(A big gulp.)* So most of the kids had gone home and it was just Celia, Jacob, and Vi left—

BIRD: —like always.

MIKA: And then I noticed Celia was hanging with me, helping clean up.

PILAR: Celia, clean up?

MIKA: Exactly. It made me wonder where Vi and Jacob were. I went to Jacob's room and the door was locked. He knows there are rules about that.

PILAR: He can't lock the door to his own room?

MIKA: Not with another boy behind it, no. *(She says boy without even realizing it. PILAR quietly clocks it.)*

BIRD: My mother had the same rule for my sister.

PILAR: That's different.

BIRD: Yeah? We don't let Vi have a cel phone in hers.

MIKA: *(Trying to steer them back to her.)* And for good reason. *(Pulling a bit of a lecture.)* Let's face it, kids are thinking about sex all the time now. I support Jacob unconditionally, but I don't have to facilitate early... activity.

PILAR: He's 12. It's not that early --

MIKA: *(Shoots her a look.)* I can be the "cool mom" without opening a Love Shack for Tween Boys.

BIRD: I should hope!

PILAR: I don't see how this applies to Vi. She's not a boy and they're not lovebirds trying to hook up.

MIKA: That's certainly not how it looked.

BIRD: How it looked?

MIKA: I do have a key, of course, and the door was open before they could get their pants up—his pants, and Vi's tail or whatever.

PILAR: They were having sex?

MIKA: No! I— I don't know exactly what they were doing, but trust me, I can be upset well short of sex.

BIRD: The little shit.

MIKA: Jacob's no worse than—

BIRD: I meant Vi. She's always riding us for setting limits and not trusting her and then she comes over here and proves us right.

MIKA: *(Relieved)* Okay then.

PILAR: Wait a minute. So they were just showing off their equipment? The way kids do—the way I did to my cousins after my older sister's quinceañera? *(To Bird)* The way you showed, what was her name, Ruthie Ann, when you were, 10 was it? I don't remember you mentioning your parents calling you a shit.

BIRD: They didn't find out — or there'd have been hell to pay.

PILAR: Too bad Vi didn't have your luck.

MIKA: *(Stunned)* I get the appeal of being Little Miss Progressive, but you are not seriously telling me you are ok with our kids doing whatever they want behind closed doors.

(PILAR doesn't answer.)

BIRD: I'm not.

PILAR: She didn't ask you. *(To MIKA.)* You know what, I am. What's going to happen? To use your term, the "boys" – yes, I heard that – aren't going to get pregnant. So what on earth is safer than playing with a best friend raised by smart people? Or do you want Jacob to start with some older guy you don't even know?

MIKA: How about Jacob doesn't start with anything yet but information and his left hand?

BIRD: Sounds about right to me.

PILAR: For god sake, both of you – they're kids. They're going to play at sex anyway.

MIKA: Not in my house.

PILAR: I respect that—

MIKA: *(Cutting her off.)* And not in yours.

BIRD: Uh huh.

MIKA: They can see each other at school and activities, obviously, but it's pretty clear we don't agree on limits, so I'd rather not set us up for more conflict.

PILAR: Can you not see that you're about to make Vi the girl of Jacob's dreams?

MIKA: It's my job to make sure she stays only in his dreams. He's 12, Pilar! I love Vi— and I *(This is a stretch.)* really enjoy you guys—but I have one kid and I'm going to do right by him even if you don't get it. That's my job.

BIRD: *(Impressed.)* Huh. *(Both women look at him. He shrugs. To MIKA.)* You're from New York—I just figured you'd out-liberal us.

PILAR: *(Chilly.)* Have you shared this edict of yours with the kids?

MIKA: Pilar—

PILAR: It should be you, right? I doubt Little Miss Progressive will say the right thing.

MIKA: *(Shoots BIRD a look.)* Bird, help me out here—

(Before he can reply, PILAR shoots him a look that says, DO NOT DARE.)

BIRD: Better just get them.

(All three exit. Black.)

End scene.

SCENE FOUR:

(Back at the Bardisa-Nickerson house. Later. VI sits in her room, wig off but nearby. She is miserable. Then she sits up and taps the air in front of her. Instantly, the MERPERSON appears; she is actually watching them on YouTube. NOTE: The actor is to be staged live, not recorded.)

MERPERSON: *(Out.)* Arise, my loves.

How special you are! How special am I!
I have a tail
that parts the waves with grace and speed.
Scales that ripple when I dive and shimmer when I surface.

I am Mer!
I am beauty and magic
and not of mere land or only sea.

Nor are you
My beautiful ones.
Not of mere land or only sea. Not of mere land or only sea.

You are beyond. You--
Are boundless.

(A shift in tone. Bright.) If you enjoyed today's Mermaid Hour, comment, "like," and share! And remember: it's not too late to submit your entry for the Be Your Own Merperson Challenge. Make a movie, make a difference!

(VI smiles, taps the air, and the MERPERSON is gone.)

(Lights up in the living room, where PILAR is obsessing over her computer, watching something online, with headphones on to keep from waking anyone. BIRD enters, watches a moment.)

BIRD: You gonna be on that thing all night?

PILAR: There's a whole series about a family like us.

BIRD: Yeah? They have an oversexed mermaid?

PILAR: It's comforting. I'm learning a lot.

BIRD: Come to bed.

PILAR: There are only four more episodes.

BIRD: Well then, you have no choice. *(PILAR turns it back on. He's a little pissed, she knows it, and he knows she knows it. But still.)* Jeezus. *(He exits.)*

(She looks briefly back toward where he'd been and watches her show. She looks content for a moment but then she learns something from the show that we can't hear and sits up straight.)

(Whatever it is, it's having a negative affect—we see it clearly in how she breathes and a look on her face that bears little of her usual confidence.)

(She stops the playback. She sits, trying to take in what she has seen. Maybe she paces. We still don't know why. But we can tell she's wrecked.)

(She sags, defeated, drops her head into her hands.)

PILAR: Goddammit.

End scene.

SCENE FIVE:

(The next day. MIKA, in expensive, of-the-moment activewear, enters with a gym bag slung over her shoulder. She has a fancy water in one hand and a smart phone in the other. Like everyone, she walks and stares at her screen. She frowns, stops, and then dials.)

MIKA: *(Her greeting is a terse staccato of three full names, never a good sign.)* Jacob. Hiro. Endo. *(Beat.)* $600 sneakers? *(Beat.)* I don't care if they're signed by Van Gogh. *(Beat.)* You better not have them on your feet and, if you do, I hope you've only walked on air, because we are going to the post office to return them right now. *(Beat.)* "Late for soccer"? I don't know whose mother you think you're talking to, but that is a complete misreading of the situation.

(She hangs up and doesn't see PILAR entering from the opposite side, looking at a stack of forms. She doesn't see MIKA either, until they're almost upon one another. Neither is delighted.)

MIKA: Pilar.

PILAR: Mika.

(Tight smiles all around.)

MIKA: Are you joining Pumped?

PILAR: *(Brays.)* Right after I win Powerball and quit my job. *(Hears herself.)* I mean—*(Beat)* My doctor's in this complex. *(Waves the forms as if they're proof.)* Not mine. Vi's.

MIKA: Eggleston, right? I've heard she's very well considered.

PILAR: She's great! She's breaking up with us but other than that—

MIKA: Breaking up?

PILAR: The doctor equivalent. "It's not you, it's me." Says she feels underqualified.

MIKA: Ah—

PILAR: Wants us to see some endocrinologist at Children's—

MIKA: Seems reasonable.

PILAR: —who doesn't know Vi! I don't want to turn her over to strangers!

MIKA: Strangers who do this for a living. *(Lecture voice.)* You just have to trust—

PILAR: You're an expert on trust? You don't even let Jacob lock his door!

MIKA: Ok—

PILAR: At least the bathroom door locks, right? He's got to masturbate somewhere.

MIKA: *(Steel.)* You've known me for all of six months. So you don't know that I'm nobody's punching bag. I get it—rough stuff going on—but I'm not your

43

difficulty. I'm going to exit gracefully now and let you rave at the next person who needs to get to the parking lot.

PILAR: Oh god—sorry. Please don't go.

MIKA: I have to get Jacob—

PILAR: Please. I'm usually the calm one on this, ok? I know that's not how it looks. *(The truth begins to spill out. MIKA chooses to stay.)* We've been headed here for years, years, right? And it's been my job to understand it, to make it ok, and it's been ok. I watched the movie with that other girl and her family and I read all the *New York Times* articles until I have a handle on things. Or I think I do, and then I read some new impossible thing. So I find a way to take that in and keep on going. Reading blogs and watching TV shows and boom, I stumble onto another thing and start again.

MIKA: Pilar—

PILAR: *(She can't stop. Out it comes.)* Like...if she does puberty blockers and hormone replacement, she'll... she'll be sterile.

MIKA: Wow.

PILAR: I asked Doctor Eggleston if that was true, and she was surprised I didn't know. It was like she was talking to a child. *(Does a doctor impression.)* "You can't skip puberty and be fertile." Isn't it wild? I hadn't, I don't know, even thought about that until a mom on TV mentioned it.

MIKA: It must have been quite a shock.

PILAR: *(Is that dig? Pilar thinks so.)* Think about everything you've had to learn about gay kids so you can help Jacob—and now imagine—*(grasping for an analogy.)* imagine discovering that when he comes out, he'll lose an eye!

MIKA: *(Takes the analogy literally.)* I don't know—an eye is visible.

PILAR: Mika!

MIKA: And I'd probably find a way to deal with it. That's how I am.

PILAR: *(Pushing ahead.)* Missing such a big detail for so long got me thinking. What else am I missing? And then I started to wonder, how many other moms like me thought they had this down to a science and then... didn't? I started googling the numbers. Do you know many parents say yes to the hormones versus how many say no? Do you?

MIKA: I'm supposed to say "no" here, right?

PILAR: Nobody knows. I looked and looked and that is a fact no one has posted. All the feel good stuff I can find. But the doubts—nobody runs the numbers on doubt.

MIKA: We're parents. Second-guessing is what we do.

PILAR: "We?" There's no "we" around here—I don't know anyone going through this.

MIKA: Well, then "I" will just go, not having any useful perspective.

PILAR: I'm sorry. I'm not like this.

MIKA: *(Acid.)* You are this week.

(MIKA exits. PILAR lets out a long sigh. Heads off the other way. End scene.)

End scene.

SCENE SIX:

(VI's room. VI wears the MERMAID costume, but looks refreshed. Her hair is her own, not the wig, and the clamshell bra is worn without a shirt. She reaches to adjust something we can't see on the iPad. She sits back. It's her turn to make a video.)

VI: Thank you for watching my entry in The Mermaid Hour "Be Your Own Merperson" Video Challenge. Please like, comment, and share. A lot.

(She finds her inner light. And begins.) I am a mermaid. My name is Violet.

Most people don't know that there's a magic time, a little blue window, when mermaids can be anything they want. Not part fish and part human, but all at once themselves: tail strong enough to walk on, lungs able to hold air and water.

When a mermaid is under the sea, she is all fish, swimming like the others, water flowing through her. But she thinks: I am not fish. I want to breathe the way the mortal humans do. When a mermaid is on land, she must give up her tail and take on legs, wobble along until it feels ok, and breathe only air, like mortals. But then she thinks: I am not mortal either.

She is happiest in the mermaid hour, the time you see her on the rock, beautiful fins sweeping across stone, her chest rising and falling with fresh air in full lungs. It's only there, where air and ocean meet, that she's everything she wants to be. No one needs her to have legs, no one wonders at the smoothness of her perfect tail.

When you see her sitting on a rock in the mermaid hour, she isn't waiting for a prince to come and make her human. She's singing a song for the sailor who will see magic in how she looks at sunset.

I am a mermaid and I have I found a sailor who sees my magic. He loves the sea like he's supposed to love the land so he knows about being caught between "should be" and "is." He saw me in the mermaid hour and said I was beautiful. When we are together, in mermaid light, atop my rock, free from land or sea, fish or mortal, we are beautiful. *You* can be beautiful! *You* can be the mermaid!

Thank you for watching my movie.

(She reaches forward about to hit pause but impulse seizes her, and she adds one more line.) I LOVE YOU JACOB ENDO!

(She taps the air in front of her. Sends her movie into the world. Behind her, we see her video projected, playing somewhere. It appears somewhere else onstage, in another spot and another, in various shapes and screens, as it crosses the internet and is shared and shared again. For a moment, VI's face lights up the world.)

End scene. (If there is an act break, it comes here.)

SCENE SEVEN:

(BIRD comes into the living room with Chinese take-out boxes, followed by PILAR with plates and a picnic blanket. They set up a picnic on the floor, usual places.)

PILAR: If they eliminate Sam Donovan, I'm going to stop watching this show forever.

BIRD: No you won't.

PILAR: We should watch that show with all the brides.

BIRD: Never. I have to draw a line somewhere.

(VI enters with another container or two and a handful of chopsticks.)

VI: Ok, Daddy, what do you call a cow with no hind legs and a long green tail?

BIRD: *(Quick.)* Moo-maid. Too easy, kid.

VI: That's what Jacob said.

PILAR: *(Opening a box.)* Scallion pancakes smell of happiness. Am I right?

(They all settle in. She hands the scallion pancake container to VI who waves it off.)

VI: You can have mine. I don't eat anything fried now.

BIRD: As of when?

PILAR: It's Chinese take out, mija. What does that leave?

VI: Garlic eggplant. *(No preamble to this.)* When do my shots start?

BIRD: *(Looking at PILAR.)* Whenever we tell ya.

PILAR: *(Shakes her head, warns him off.)* Eggleston can't even see us again till December.

VI: That's like forever!

PILAR: *(Clicking in our direction.)* Show's on.

VI: Mami—

PILAR: Talk to me at commercial.

(They eat and watch TV. We hear indistinguishable TV noise. A ringing cell phone interrupts but they ignore at first. Phone keeps ringing and PILAR rises and pauses the TV we can't see.)

VI: Don't stop it!

PILAR: It's just paused.

BIRD: Leave it.

PILAR: What if it's an emergency?

(She exits.)

BIRD: *(To VI.)* If it's an emergency, why call us?

VI: I know, right? *(They laugh together, partners in crime.)*

(PILAR comes back, looking concerned. Speaking into phone.)

PILAR: This was where? *(VI truly doesn't get that this is about her. BIRD sits up, cocked for trouble.)* Tell me again what she said. *(Beat. Now VI is on alert too.)* 180,000 views?

(VI gets it. Knows she has misfired.)

BIRD: What is she talking about? *(VI hides her face.)* What did you do?

PILAR: Of course. We'll talk tomorrow. Thank you for letting me know. *(Hangs up. Takes a breath.)*

BIRD: What?

VI: It was a challenge! *(Quoting a slogan.)* "Make a movie, make a difference!"

PILAR: Our daughter put a half-dressed video of herself on YouTube.

VI: I was fully dressed—in a costume you made!

BIRD: Doing what?

PILAR: Telling the world she's a mermaid.

BIRD: *(So?)* Ok...

PILAR: And that she loves Jacob and he loves her body.

VI: I didn't say that! Not that way!

PILAR: That's how Mika took it, and that's how it sounded to the relatives in Japan who saw it first and told her about it.

BIRD: Aw, Christ.

PILAR: Apparently, Mermaid Girl is sweeping the internet as a touching cry for tolerance and understanding. Not that her own parents have seen it.

VI: It was for kids like me.

PILAR: Yeah? Now it's for everyone. Your school. The nursing home. Daddy's jobs. Jacob's grandparents in Tokyo.

VI: I just wanted—

PILAR: To show off that top. To get your way. Don't try and play innocent now—

BIRD: What does *that* mean?

VI: Yeah!

PILAR: Talking of rainbow parties and trying to sneak out in a bra – you posted this to the whole world because you can't stop and think twice about anything you do. You're just this walking fireball of impulse who does what she wants.

BIRD: *(Surprised.)* Uh, you might be overshooting here.

PILAR: You want her all over the internet?

BIRD: I mean, we haven't seen it.

PILAR: Well Mika has and, guess what? Jacob can't have anything to do with you now.

VI: But I'm almost his girlfriend!

PILAR: As far as his mom's concerned, you're a delusional boy who dresses up like a mermaid.

BIRD: *(Pissed.)* She said that?

PILAR: Exact words.

VI: When I get my shots she'll see. I'm not a boy.

BIRD: Fuck her.

VI: It's your fault for making me wait so long.

PILAR: My fault!

VI: *(Getting increasingly ramped up.)* I want to start now! I don't want to wait till Christmas!

PILAR: I never said you're getting them at all.

VI: You did! You did!

PILAR: You heard what you wanted. I said we'd talk when you were ready and as far as I can tell, you're anything but ready to be trusted with a big decision.

VI: *(Frantic.)* Daddy! *(Runs to him.)* Say something to her! *(BIRD is stuck. He's getting the delay he wants but he has no idea why, and he doesn't want to argue.)* Daddy please!

BIRD: I—Uh—

VI: Daddy!

PILAR: One problem at a time. I think we need to watch the video. *(Finds YouTube on her phone.)*

VI: *(Crying.)* You promised Mami.

(PILAR starts the video and BIRD watches. We see the video still on the back wall.)

VI's VOICE projected: I am a mermaid. My name is Violet. This is my story.

VI: *(Crying.)* You promised. You promised! *(Runs off.)*

BIRD: What the hell just happened?

PILAR: She's a mess. You try and be a good parent, you try and teach responsibility and common sense, and nothing—none of it sticks.

BIRD: No. What's with "you don't deserve shots"?

PILAR: Is that a problem? You didn't want her to get them!

BIRD: I never said that! And forget me—What's going on with you?

PILAR: Maybe you were right. Maybe I'm rushing this.

BIRD: Didn't you just see Eggleston?

PILAR: Yes.

BIRD: So—what does she say about timing?

PILAR: *(Ignores this.)* Vi ...*(A breath.)* Could end up sterile.

BIRD: Yeah? *(Waits.)*

PILAR: That's it? "Yeah?"

BIRD: It's not like you thought she'd be making babies in there. *(A beat. PILAR burns a little. He enjoys having thought of this before she did. He enjoys it a lot.)* I mean—

PILAR: Do. Not. *(Hand up.)* I'm a CNA and I'm working on being a nurse and it's only thanks to me ever reading a textbook that you have any clue what is going on with the only child we have, so back up, querrido. Like there wasn't already a lot to think about with negotiating her bathroom at school and playing soccer and changing for swim lessons. Maybe I hadn't thought about babies or any of that because there's fucking plenty on my plate just getting us from minute to minute.

BIRD: You're alone on this now?

PILAR: I work overtime and still do all the pick-ups—

BIRD: I have two jobs and still do the drop-offs!

PILAR: And cook every weeknight except TV Picnic—

BIRD: I make all the lunches!

PILAR: *(Trump card.)* And handle all, *all* of the our-boy-is-a-girl stuff with her doctor and the school and the other parents.

BIRD: So…she's impulsive and I'm not enough help and your life sucks. *(Raises beer.)* Here's to you.

PILAR: *(Not giving in.)* Don't talk to me like I'm stupid and I won't bitch about my life. *(It's quiet for a couple of awkward beats. They just sit. She relents a little but not quickly or entirely.)* I just can't believe I missed this. I've pictured her as a bride. As a mom. As a grandmother—can you believe it?

BIRD: Well, yeah. I mean, she's gonna want the whole ride. But it's not like she needs to make a baby for any of it.

PILAR: I guess.

BIRD: Hell, maybe by the time she's ready, they'll figure out a way—fake womb or something!

PILAR: A fake womb!

BIRD: *(Defensive.)* I mean, if women have room for one, why wouldn't a guy? When I was her age, I'd never heard of any of this—the surgery, the shots, the other shots. If you'd told me then, I'd have thought it was like Dr. Who or something. But look, here we are. So, why not a fake womb?

PILAR: *(Rolling her eyes.)* Yeah, why not? *(She starts gathering the Chinese food boxes.)*

BIRD: So that's it? No shots?

PILAR: I don't know.

BIRD: If ya don't know, maybe don't go shooting your mouth off in front of Vi until you do.

PILAR: Do you hear yourself? How you're laying it on me, like I've got to figure it out for all of us? You just get to show up and blame me for whatever choice gets made.

BIRD: Ya think?

PILAR: And the worst thing is, I buy into it. I tell myself, this is on me. *(BIRD looks like he'll speak. She cuts him off.)* Yes, you do a lot, but I *rock* being a mom. And I always have. No matter how I screw up moment to moment, I've always been able to step back and say: look at my happy, smart, sensitive kid. More than our marriage, more than work, I've gotten this right…and I don't want to blow it. I'm used to having clarity and, right now… *(Let's the thought fall.)* I have the number for Children's. I just can't bring myself to dial it.

BIRD: *(A little pissed at that speech. Trying to tamp it down.)* She's gonna hate you for a while.

PILAR: Yeah, well, enjoy it. You get to be good cop now.

BIRD: I don't know about that.

(VI appears, in jammies. She has been crying. She doesn't look at PILAR.)

VI: Daddy. Can you lay on my bed till I fall asleep?

BIRD: You know it.

PILAR: Do you want some water, mija?

VI: *(Ignores her entirely.)* Come, daddy.

(She extends a miserable hand and he takes it. They exit.)

(PILAR is left alone. She stands there a moment, then takes the Chinese food and leaves.)

End scene.

SCENE EIGHT:

(MIKA's house. MIKA and BIRD enter. She has a beer for him and wine for herself.)

MIKA: Thanks for coming. I'm sorry about how I handled the video.

BIRD: Yeah, I'm thinking the principal really didn't need to see that.

MIKA: "I'm sorry" means that I know that already. This is an apology.

BIRD: And this is me being a dick because I'm stressed and tired. So, thanks, I appreciate it.

MIKA: *(Sighs.)* I feel like I learned so much about gay this and gay that in the last year, and I just wanted to get a handle on that, when along comes this. Vi got all the stuff I didn't blast Jacob with.

BIRD: Ok.

MIKA: The idea of my gay son with the trans girl—I'm not an awful person, but my head imploded for a moment, ok? *(Beat.)* It was more than that. It was his name—she used his name. That was the first gift we gave him. And suddenly it was hers to define? It changed what it meant, how people might see him.

BIRD: *(She doesn't get that she's misfiring here.)* I, uh…I know plenty about lost names.

59

MIKA: Right. *(Ouch. Beat.)* I don't want to admit this, but…there was a piece to it of shame, not for him, but for me: in not knowing about the video first, of hearing it from grandparents who don't come from a culture or time in which even who Jacob is would be allowed, much less—*(Wants to say VI but doesn't.)*

BIRD: Yeah.

MIKA: I thought, gay is enough for a kid in this world, if I can un-associate Jacob from this transgender "mermaid" business, it would protect him from further insult.

BIRD: *(Surprised.)* Your son's like the most popular kid in school.

MIKA: *(Dismissing this.)* Only because he's new and he carries the caché of Manhattan.

BIRD: Exactly. None of them give a shit he's gay. My day, he'd have been knocked around the lockers at very least.

MIKA: That still happens.

BIRD: Here? You're protecting him from our childhood.

MIKA: Bird—

BIRD: *(Cuts her off.)* Which I get.

MIKA: You do?

BIRD: It's too next world, right? Like, it's already here, but, *jeez*. Whatever Vi and Jacob think of it, it's just so far beyond. I spend all my time playing catch up.

MIKA: I had no idea. You seem to have a handle on this.

BIRD: *(Sips quietly.)* You're a parent. You oughta know better than "seems."

MIKA: Fair enough. *(Clinks his glass.)*

BIRD: It's not the life I ever saw, you know, in my head. *(A big swig.)* So I always had this dream that I would have season tickets to Fenway and take my boys to all the games. Who knows why only boys—Pilar would say it's sexist to make it boys because it's sports, but it isn't sexist to just see a thing in your head. It's not like I'm ever gonna have season tickets on what I make, anyway, so it's just a dream, and dreams make their own shape, right?

When Victor was born *[If actor playing VI is not ethnically akin to either parent, simply switch line to adoption-friendly "when we adopted."]*, I was like, I'm on my way. But Vic was it. One and done, that's that. And when he was little, I heard from a friend that he had a buddy with season tickets who kinda made a time share out of the seats. Bleacher seats—section 42— which I love, cause the view of the field is awesome, and you can see every scoreboard. The dates were shit— April nights and August afternoons—but I didn't care. I was like, this is it: Me and Vic, we can taste the dream.

Vic was four and it was pretty much the first night he ever got to stay up late. I knew he wouldn't make it through the game, but I was cool because it was just the beginning. Pilar didn't come— Sox aren't her thing, which is fine by me, cause I don't want to go to my church, which is what Fenway is, and worry about someone not liking it.

And Vic, he loves it. For all the wrong reasons: the lights are pretty and the TVs are so big and the singalong—that's what he calls Sweet Caroline in the 8th—is awesome! Can't follow the game even though I'm trying to explain and doesn't seem to care, but he's so happy to be there, I'm like: *Win*. This is what it means to be a parent: make your kid happy and be happy doing it. I let him eat a hot dog AND fries AND ice cream AND soda. Pilar woulda ripped me a new one if she could see all that junk, but it's four games a summer, and summer comes just once a year.

Next season, same thing— he loves it, win or lose, can't wait to go. Starts to understand the game a little, so he gets why I'm screaming and shouting. It's not quite the way I imagined, like when he's standing on the seat shaking his butt to the music, but it's great, and it's ours.

Until six.

Six. The year of all the towels on his head for long hair and every bed sheet and throw making a dress or a train. That year...Well, you take your son to Fenway in his favorite purple hoodie with all the rhinestone butterflies, and see how that goes. I could feel the other dads, their sympathy, just boring thru me, "Wow that kid is wicked gay." Some even gave me the look, like, "Dude, I feel your pain." And I just tried to let it roll off. I did. I knew there'd be looks when we left the house and I didn't say he couldn't wear it, cause I'm a good dad, a Democrat dad.

Until we hit the friggin pink jersey store. Victor sees the pink crap—and gets possessed. Like, has to have it. Has to. Right then. Please daddy, I want one. Pleeeeease.

And I say no, not because I'm an asshole. Pink jerseys— and pink caps—they're a crime on their own merits. We're RED SOX, it's in the friggin' name.

Anyway, I say no pink jersey, and he loses it. Bursts into tears. Think my son looks gay with his sparkly hoodie? Now add weeping and moaning, "I want the pink one! I want the pink one!" And then over and over, "I need it! I need it!"

So, I'm trying to get him outta there and he's sitting in the middle of the friggin' floor and it's a scene, right? And I'm pissed: you don't cry to get your way. But he won't stop. I end up shouting. "Why the fuck do you need a pink shirt?" Just like that I am a bad parent cause I'm not just yelling at my kid in public, but swearing. Father of the year.

Vic starts shouting over me just to be heard, and then forgetting me, this crazy shrieking, "Because I'm a girl! I'm a girl! I'm a girl."

(Visceral. Losing himself.) And I say, "Get up. Get up off the floor. You don't get what you want this way!" And I start pulling his arm, pretty hard, which makes the crying worse.

And then this guy, twice my size, tatts up his neck, takes my arm to stop me, and I swear I am going to punch him cause I need to punch something, I'm so frustrated and embarrassed and freaked out. But he looks me in the eye, and I see he's just trying to watch out for me, and he says, "You are man enough to get your kid that shirt and your kid's gonna love you forever if you do."

Only in Massachusetts, right?

So I stand there, not punching anything and not yanking Vic's arm, and a vein in my forehead is throbbing so hard I'm gonna go blind, and fuck it, I buy the shirt. But not for him. For me—to stop the scene, to stop everyone from looking, to just get out of there. And Vic knows, he knows this, so he holds the shirt close like a blanket but doesn't dare to put it on. He whispers thank you and follows me back to our seat and his face is red with the shame of winning, and I see this and it's misery. But I can't bring myself to make him feel better, because I know right then. That it isn't just gonna be towels and bedsheets forever.

So I sit there, staring at the field, the boys in white running around being boys like my boy never will be, and I think, "Here it comes. Here it all comes."

At the seventh inning stretch, Vic asks if he can put on the jersey if he wears the hoodie over it so no one will see. Like the hoodie's so butch, right? His voice is so shy, so small, I'm like Christ, he's scared to death of me. So I do what Pilar would've done to start with. I say, "Go for it." And he does, changing right there in the seat. When he starts to put the hoodie over the pink to hide it—I stop him. Don't make a big deal, just swallow hard and say, "Ah, skip it. Too hot for all that."

Kid just glows, glows like a friggin star, the rest of that game. Then sleeps in the shirt for the next three nights before Pilar snags it for the wash.

This year, when Vi told that story to Dr. Eggleston, she left out the bit in the store. She told it as the happiest day of that whole year, because I let her be who she was. Can ya stand it? She tells this as a good dad story.

I wanna be proud of me for that, but, course, I know how I acted. (Beat) No. That's not it. I wanna be proud of myself, but...sometimes, when we go to games now, I can't help but look over at my daughter, who I love with my whole breaking heart, and still, I think, this, this is where I lost my son.

(He stops. It is perfectly quiet. MIKA is in tears.) Too much, huh?

MIKA: Not at all. *(Trying to get herself back.)* Tattoo guy...in the story...

BIRD: Yeah?

MIKA: I bet he didn't have kids.

BIRD: No one giving parenting advice ever does.

(They clink beers on that.)

MIKA: It's funny to hear you talk about Vi as "he."

BIRD: Tell me about it. The pronoun thing is killer. When I'm pissed, I never know whether to tell her she's acting like a dick or a bitch. Pardon my language.

MIKA: Pardoned. But I actually just meant, well, I've only ever known the girl.

BIRD: Uh, I'm thinking you called her "a delusional boy" just like two days ago.

MIKA: You just called her a bitch so let's not judge what a person says in the heat of the moment. *(JACOB appears.)* What's up honey?

JACOB: I want to go see Vi. Can that be ok again?

MIKA: For now. As long as the door stays open. *(JACOB rolls his eyes.)* Some rules still apply.

BIRD: Fine by me. But not tonight—I'm a little done. *(Hands back beer. To JACOB.)* Tomorrow after school. You can walk her home.

(All three exit.)

End scene.

SCENE NINE:

(Vi's room. The next day.)

JACOB: *(Handing over a duffel bag.)* They're not gonna fit. I mean, look at you.

(VI digs through stuff—it's Jacob's clothes. She's miserable. She holds up a pair of jeans. They don't look like a good call but she wriggles into them anyway.)

JACOB (cont.): You don't wear jeans.

(VI shoots him a look and rolls her eyes. She pulls on a long-sleeved graphic tee or men's hoodie.)

JACOB (cont.): *(Made defensive by the silent treatment.)* Mom said I couldn't come before. No need to be pissed at me. And it's not like I made a video declaring my love for you so all of Japan could hear it.

VI: *(Stopping with the clothes. Very small.)* Sorry.

JACOB: You totally screwed up my chances with Xander.

VI: *(Confused)* The student teacher?

JACOB: I could tell he thought was I cute.

VI: Ewwww!

JACOB: Now he thinks I have a girlfriend. *(Not looking.)* I like boys, Vi.

(VI stands up in her new outfit. Tries to change her stance at little. It's clear that she's trying on boy as a pose.)

(JACOB looks at her, then looks away. Firm shake of his head. His reply is clear too: no, she's not a boy. She pulls the new stuff off and curls up, miserable.)

JACOB (cont.): Do you ever wish you could smoke? When mom feels this way, she totally smokes. It's like unfair that we can't. *(He sees she is wounded. Goes to sit next to her.)* I like you as you, Vi. I don't "like you" like you cause I like boys but I wouldn't want you to be a boy because then you wouldn't be you. You're lit, Vi. Just as you are. K? *(Nothing.)* You're a girl and I'm gay – we're supposed to have each other's backs. *(Selling it.)* It was in *Teen Vogue* – I'm the gay best friend. You have to have one.

VI: *(Flat.)* Ok.

JACOB: *(Beat.)* You looked pretty on YouTube.

VI: I don't want to talk about it.

JACOB: We could make more videos—girl power and stuff. You could be huge.

VI: *(This only makes it worse.)* Daddy took away my iPad privileges and I can only use the phone in the living room and if they're present. *(Sags. Tired.)* Can you go home now?

JACOB: *(He's used to running the show and feeling her adoration so this is killing him.)* Yeah. *(Tries to find something to lighten the mood. Gets up on one knee, faux proposal.)* Vi, will you be my Merfriend? *(She doesn't look up, so he takes her hand and kisses it, very sweetly. She reacts as if burned, snatching it away and burying her face in both hands. Not what he expected. He rises.)* Uh, ok. See you.

(He exits. She cries. After a minute, she pulls out the iPad she's not allowed to have. She glances at the door to make sure she won't get caught. She hits play.)

MERPERSON: *(Out.)* Arise, my loves.
How free we are If we choose to be.
I choose! I choose!

Should waves confine me I breach
Should the earth restrain me I leap

Gravity requires weight
And my spirit is light
I cannot be pulled down
I cannot be sucked under

Not of mere land or only sea, Nothing to be contained

I'm free if I choose to be
Choose, children to be
Choose to be
Free!

(MERPERSON disappears and VI looks positively fierce. She taps on her IPAD and then types a note.)

VI: "Should earth restrain me—I leap."
(She runs off.)

End scene.

SCENE TEN:

(A few hours later. PILAR enters with arms full of grocery bags, awkward to manage, and her phone ringing in one of them.)

PILAR: *(Shouting in the direction of VI's room.)* Mija— come help me. *(The phone continues to ring. She sets down the bags, spilling items, including cans of GOYA black beans. Tries to catch the rolling cans. Shouting off again.)* You're killing your Mami with this attitude! *(Digs around for the phone with her free hand. Into the phone.)* Hello? Oh—*(Her tone gets quite chilly.)* Mika. *(Beat.)* I didn't even know she asked for his clothes—of course we'll return them. *(Beat.)* You got them in Soho, I know, they're better than Boston jeans. *(Beat.)* I'm not picking a fight, I'm picking up beans. Goodbye. *(Hangs up.)*

(She rises and heads for VI's room.) Jacob wants his fancy jeans back. And I want some help out here. *(Irked, she heads off and then immediately back on.)*

PILAR (cont.): Vi? VI! *(She exits as if to search other rooms, and we hear her calling out, getting frantic. Repeating from off.)* Mija? Mija! *Mija!*

(When she re-enters, she has the iPad clutched like a talisman. She races out the front door.)

(Whenever VI appears, we get city noise and can watch her growing realization that this wasn't the best impulse of her already impulsive youth. She will move from place to place around the stage, sometimes exiting completely

between her beats. The other characters will be appearing around the stage in their imagined various locales, without sets, and will not see VI. They are communicating by phone call and text.)

(Stage directions and dialogue for VI's escape to the city will alternate with others' dialogue back in her hometown. As a general note, the motion needs to keep spinning forward here, the pace adding to the fears that ramp up for her and her family both Until Crux appears.)

(Accompanied by subway and crowd sounds, VI enters. She stares at her phone, looks around, starts across the stage. She stops. Steps back the way she came. Reconsiders. Continues forward the way she had been going.)

PILAR: I need to report a missing child. Not stolen. Missing—*(It hurts to say this.)* a run-away.
(Defensive.) It's only been a few hours I guess—whenever school got out, but–*(Incensed at being asked how she knows VI is actually missing.)* ONE: She's 12 so she doesn't get to just wander off without telling me and TWO: Because she left a fucking note. That's how.

*(VI has her eyes on her phone and is focused on a map she is following until we hear a blaring car horn and screech of tires. She jumps back, clearly having almost walked into traffic.
She is shaking. She takes a few deep breaths to calm herself. Shoulders up, she looks around, then heads counterintuitively away from the direction she had started.)*

(MIKA, JACOB, and PILAR appear separately.)

MIKA: *(Answering phone call from PILAR.)* This is Mika. *(Beat.)* What? No—I have no idea. I hardly think she'd come running to me and per usual Jacob hasn't said anything.

PILAR: If she's in New York City, it's because your son convinced her it's the promised land!

(PILAR hangs up and MIKA texts JACOB.)

JACOB: *(Answering a text from his mom.)* Help her run away? God mom, as if!

(VI looks miserable. She is completely turned around. She walks more hesitantly. Looks back over her shoulder. Hurries a little more. Looks over her shoulder. We hear teasing voices or jeering. They should be scary. She pulls out a whistle and blows it for all she's worth to ward off someone we can't see, then runs off fast as she can, as we hear laughter from older youths.)

(BIRD appears in Home Depot apron, answering a call from PILAR.)

BIRD: Did she *say* New York or you *think* New York? Jeezus! We have to call the po—*(She cuts him off.)* You called them first? *(Listens.) And* Jacob? Christ, Peel, what if she'd been with me? I'm on my way. *(Hangs up. Furious mutter.)* Not that you missed me.

VI: *(Scared beyond measure. Trembling, dials a number on her cell.)* Hi...I...um, I'm trying to find you guys, but I'm kinda lost, and I'm freaked out, and can you, uh, can you just get me?

(Looking around.) Desi's Market and, uh, a gas station. There are a lot of boys hanging out there and I'm alone... *(Her voice cracks.)* My parents? They think I'm in New York.

PILAR: *(On phone with police.)* You really can't look until-- *(Hears a reply.)* Of course I'll stay by the phone. *(Hangs up.)*

BIRD: *(To PILAR.)* Anything? *(She shakes her head.)* What the fuck, Peel?

PILAR: *(Ready to have a target to attack.)* If anything happens to Vi, I will never forgive us. But if you put this all on me, I will never forgive you!

(Lights up on VI show her sitting, knees hugged to chest, head tucked down, as CRUX enters. They are the actor from the MERPERSON YouTube videos, genderqueer, and dressed pretty much like a lot of lefty grad students in Boston—a well-worn leather jacket over a graphic t-shirt, with cool jeans and boots, and whatever accessories [jewelry, tattoos, piercing] suit them. CRUX has to walk a fine line between warm, wary of being alone with a child in this situation, and being afraid: they're a gender nonconfirming person out on a tough corner in the dark.)

CRUX: *(Kneeling next to her.)* Vi? Is that you in there? *(VI throws herself on CRUX, crying, relieved and scared and tired.)* Okay...We have to talk about boundaries at some point, but...you're safe. Which is kind of remarkable for this corner after dark. *(CRUX rises extends a hand. VI gets up, biting her lip.)*

73

CRUX: *(Gently.)* We have to get you home to your folks. *(VI covers her face.)* I know, I know. But, truly, if a stranger from the internet offered to take you anywhere else…Vi, you can't even imagine.

(They exit.)

(PILAR, MIKA, and JACOB appear in their own lights.)

PILAR: *(To MIKA.)* She's ok. They're bringing her home.

MIKA: *(This all only proves she was right to want less VI in her life.)* I'll be sure to tell Jacob.

(PILAR and MIKA exit.)

JACOB: *(Texting.)* That was a shitty thing to do, Vi. NOT COOL. *(Hits send.)*

(Exits.)

End scene.

SCENE ELEVEN:

(Later at the house. BIRD paces.)

BIRD: Are they ever gonna make it?

PILAR: It's an hour drive from Boston even when there isn't road work.

BIRD: How the fuck did she even get there?

PILAR: What matters is that she's on her way. And that it was a social worker who found her in the first place.

BIRD: So we got an interrogation coming.

PILAR: *(Confused.)* What?

BIRD: From the social worker. And you know the police will follow up. The whole fuckin' world in our business.

PILAR: Bird! *(He stops.)* Just—

(PILAR bursts into tears. This surprises BIRD to a degree but he does the exact right thing: he holds her. For a moment they just stand that way. Finally, BIRD pulls away carefully.)

BIRD: You think she's alright?

PILAR: *(Still imagining.)* She could have—anything could have— *(Tries to shake off the vision. A breath.)* But according to Crux—

BIRD*: (City people!)* Crux is a name?

PILAR: —that's who found her. And according to Crux, Vi's fine.

BIRD: A social worker would know, yeah?

PILAR: I guess so.

BIRD: So I can breathe out and be pissed now?

PILAR: What?

BIRD: Cause I can't keep up with this crap.

PILAR: Bird—

BIRD: I can't. I want to do the right thing, whatever that is, and she won't give us a friggin' half second to figure it out. The sex talk and the video and now—it's like she's driving this ship and doesn't care that we're supposed to be at the wheel. I get why the witch stuck Rapunzel in a tower—it was for her own damn good. *(Beat.)* God I sound like a shit.

PILAR: Kinda.

BIRD: I just took off from work when you called, racing here, thinking, please God, don't let someone hurt her, and all the way beating myself up for failing her, for not getting my arms around this better. But now she's on the way and everything's gonna be fine or fine-ish, and suddenly I want to shake her and shout at her like a crazy man. *(Beat.)* I can't be that guy. When she gets home, I need to be the dad who can't live without her.

PILAR: *(She hesitates. Her voice catches. She has to say this.)* She really wants those shots.

BIRD: Are you kidding? I don't want a kid who takes off making decisions like that.

PILAR: I don't want her taking off because we won't let her make decisions.

BIRD: *(Groans.)* I'm losing my fucking mind.

PILAR: I called Children's...*(He looks surprised.)* There's no WebMD for this. Might as well bring in the big guns.

BIRD: Good: Let her make them crazy.

PILAR: They can't get her in till the new year.

BIRD: Yeah, well, I don't think anyone wants to meet me right this second.

PILAR: As long as they do meet you. You have to come with me.

BIRD: So now I'm invited?

PILAR: *(Rising to the bait.)* You never needed an invitation to—*(This is the oldest argument. Stops herself.)* We have to work on this as a team.

BIRD: That's a two-way street.

PILAR: *(Baring the truth.)* It didn't used to feel like such a chore to take each other seriously. We have to do that again. And better. *(A direct look in his eyes.)*

BIRD: *(Hard to hold her eyes—they're rusty at this. But he does. Then breaks the look. Then looks back, a little embarrassed.)* It's weird to talk about us. It's been all-Vi-all-the-time for so long.

PILAR: That's how she likes it.

BIRD: Right? *(Beat. Breathes out.)* Jeez, Peel. What'm I gonna say to her?

PILAR: Just, go easy—

(CRUX and VI arrive. VI is sheepish, hangs back. PILAR goes to VI and hugs her instantly. BIRD is thrown by the presence of CRUX. He doesn't go to VI yet.)

PILAR: *(To VI)* Are you ok? *(VI doesn't speak yet. PILAR addresses CRUX.)* Thank you for bringing her.

(VI pulls away from PILAR, looking at BIRD.)

VI: *(Embarrassed. Especially worried about her dad.)* Are you…are you mad at me?

PILAR: Oh mija—

VI: Daddy?

BIRD: *(He gives PILAR a look for support. Finds the right guy inside. But it's not easy.)* No, honey. *(Adjusts.)* Yeah, yeah I am. But come on. You're still my girl.

(He opens his arms.)

End scene.

SCENE TWELVE:

(A bit later. PILAR is alone with a beer, when CRUX enters. PILAR doesn't greet them. Awkward.)

CRUX: *(As PILAR just sips her beer.)* I should head out soon. Any last questions, fire away.

PILAR: Ok. *(Takes a swig. Has been simmering. Blunt.)* Why you?

CRUX: You mean—

PILAR: Why did my child run off to a stranger?

CRUX: She doesn't think of me that way. I'm a YouTuber vlogger—

PILAR: "Vlogger?"

CRUX: *(Trying to use language she'll get.)* Like a performer.

PILAR: What happened to "social worker?"

CRUX: Working on that. I march in June. MCN is my last placement.

PILAR: Am I supposed to know what that means?

CRUX: MCN? *(Spelling it out.)* Mermaid Charity Network.

PILAR: That sounds ridiculous.

CRUX: We work with transgender, genderqueer, and binary-resistant kids...

PILAR: You collect 12-year-olds?

CRUX: Most clients come through clinical referrals. But your daughter...she saw our website and just showed up.

PILAR: That's Vi, alright. *(Beat.)* So you do what exactly on YouTube?

CRUX: Inspirational performance pieces. They're meant to be empowering.

PILAR: Oh, it is—you got her making videos.

CRUX: She showed me her channel.

PILAR: *(Hand up to stop him. Shaking her head.)* She's a channel. You're a network. What a world! *(Blunt.)* Are you trans? Or "genderqueer"?

CRUX: *(Very gentle teasing.)* Not obvious, huh?

PILAR: *(Just motions head to toe at CRUX's look.)* Let's go with no.

CRUX: I'm...Crux. *(A smile.)* I've never been into easy definitions.

PILAR: Then I guess you've come to the right place.

CRUX: About her video for our Merperson Challenge...

PILAR: Please—

CRUX: Have you seen it?

PILAR: Is that a serious question?

CRUX: It's inspiring. It's beautiful. Her video made—

PILAR: *(Interjecting.)*—her a target! *(Paces.)* It made them both targets! Who tells kids to put their private lives on the internet? *(The sting of truth in that hits CRUX a little.)* What kid needs to invite the whole world into their mess? *(She hears how that sounds.)* I don't mean—*(Mess? Maybe she does. Maybe she doesn't. Just gives up.)*

CRUX: *(Really feeling her distress.)* I'm so sorry... *(Extends a hand to squeeze her arm sympathetically, but she shrugs it off and steps away.)*

PILAR: Tell me: What did your parents do?

CRUX: Well...

PILAR: Did they go the whole nine yards or did you have to wait until you were on your own to do...whatever you have or haven't done?

CRUX: I haven't spoken to my parents since I was a child. And that was a long time ago. *(A brief pause.)* It would have been nice to have them involved. *(Seizing on the moment.)* Vi wants you involved. She just freaked out a little. Kids do that. *(Produces some material from a bag.)* I have to get back to the city. But I brought some of our materials.

PILAR: Pamphlets, really? Hasn't the internet killed these things yet?

CRUX: Not everyone has equal access to the web. Some people—

PILAR: *(Cuts them off.)* Are better off that way! My god, the internet's insane. *(A half beat.)* I keep swapping studies I don't like for ones that will make me feel better. *(Hands back the pamphlets.)* I can't read another thing.

CRUX: *(Slides one pamphlet closer.)* Well, at least look at the one on grief. *(Gently.)* It's ok to mourn what you feel you've lost, even something you wished for and never had. *(This lands for PILAR who cannot even meet CRUX's eyes. CRUX rises to go.)* Just…Can I tell you, before I go, that I haven't seen a lot of educators or experts, much less kids, who capture this experience as well as your daughter did in a two-minute video challenge? Vi is pretty magical.

PILAR: *(Affronted.)* You hardly need to tell me. I know. *(Softens.)* I know.

CRUX: Then go with that.

(CRUX gives her a little hug which she reluctantly accepts, then exits. BIRD passes CRUX on the way. They just nod at each other and keep going.)

BIRD: Vi's out like rock. *(Beat.)* So what did, uh…they say? *(Pleased with himself.)* Huh—I nailed the pronoun, first try.

PILAR: Sorry, there's no medal for that. *(Indicates the stack.)* They left pamphlets.

BIRD: Wow. These would be great to start a fire. *(This wins a tired smile from PILAR.)* Hey. You know how when Vic was a baby we'd go look at him sleeping and just stand there, all quiet, and so focused it was kinda creepy? *(She smiles at the memory.)* Let's go be creepy.

PILAR: Now? If she wakes up—we really will look creepy.

BIRD: I'm ok with that. She could stand to be a little scared of us.

(Lights fade as they head for her room.)

End scene.

SCENE THIRTEEN:

(In the new year. Maybe some cheesy valentine decorations. BIRD comes out and starts setting up TV picnic, arranging the boxes and plates. PILAR finally enters with wine for herself and a beer for BIRD. She sits opposite him with space in between for VI. BIRD glances past her into the house.)

BIRD: What's she doing in there?

PILAR: Make-up.

BIRD: For TV picnic? You're kidding me.

PILAR: *(Doing a terrific impression.)* "I'm 12 Mami, it's what you do when you're 12."

BIRD: And you encouraged this?

PILAR: *(Shrugs.)* I don't want her getting make-up tips from Celia, right? *(The image makes him shudder noticeably.)*

BIRD: Like she needs to stand out more. *(Beat.)* My buddy at work—you know Andy, yeah? He saw the YouTube.

PILAR: How? Why?

BIRD: One of his boys saw it in health class – some girl did a presentation on it. And Andy's kid showed him.

PILAR: What did he say?

BIRD: Said Vi has a way with words – we must be proud.

PILAR: *(A little shamed.)* Please tell me you said "we loved" it.

BIRD: *(No. That's not what he said.)* Uh, more or less. *(He looks to make sure VI is not on her way in.)* I don't see much change since the blocker thing.

PILAR: That's the whole point!

BIRD: I mean...*(A sigh.)* Things feel almost normal again. Like, what's the big deal? And then I remember and jeez, it hits me in the gut. And my wheels start spinning and I'm thinking about the shots down the road and the stuff after that—*(Groans.)*

PILAR: She could go the Crux route and skip all of it. That's a thing now.

BIRD: *(Half kidding.)* Don't even. I finally tell all the guys at work the whole deal—now I'm gonna go in and say she's a they?

PILAR: *(An eyebrow.)* The needs of the Home Depot lunch room are just about her last concern.

(Vi enters.)

BIRD: Nice make-up, kiddo!

VI: *(She can't believe he's such a moron.)* Daddy! I washed it all off. It looked stupid. *(Sees boxes.)* A *small* order of scallion pancakes?

PILAR: You don't eat fried things!

VI: *(The universe hates her.)* Oh my god, that was November! *(Grabs the box. Ridiculously forlorn.)* I love scallion pancakes...

(BIRD and PILAR shoot each other puzzled looks.)

BIRD: What's up?

VI: Nothing! *(But she really wants to talk about it.)*

PILAR: Something up at school?

VI: No....*(Small voice.)* Except Jacob is still avoiding me.

BIRD: I friggin' hate that kid.

VI: Daddy!

PILAR: I think his mom has something to do with it.

VI: No, it's...I really freaked him out by taking off. *(This is a door, opening a little.)*

BIRD: *(Gentle dig.)* Just him?

VI: *(Groan.)* Are you guys ever gonna relax?

(They hesitate a beat too long.)

BIRD: I'd say the odds aren't good. *(We hear TV noise.)* Show's on.

PILAR: What's this week?

VI: Prom dress challenge.

BIRD: You love this one.

VI: *(She doesn't say anything in reply at first. Somehow there's more to it.)* Do you think...*(Stops. Clearly wants to say more.)*

PILAR: What, sweetie?

VI: ...I'll go to prom?

(It costs her to ask. She can see the whole dream. The following lines build and blossom with her imagining the gorgeousness of possibility, but should also ache with longing from the painful undercurrent of knowing it might not be hers, so that her last words are as much wistful as hopeful.)

VI (cont.): That maybe...by then...the old days will be so long ago and so many schools ago no one will know any me but Violet? And a boy will ask me and I'll say yes and we'll get all dressed up and I can be like a girl in a movie, getting flowers and taking pictures and standing up in the sunroof of a rented limo, and just...*happy?*

PILAR: *(Lord: so many emotions. None easy. But she gives the answer she wishes and the only answer she dares at this moment.)* Querrida...of course you will.

BIRD: Your date lays a finger on you, I'm gonna end him.

VI: Daddy! *(Grabs the scallion pancakes box.)*

PILAR: So you're that kind of dad?

BIRD: Yes, I am.

VI: *(Scrunched up face.)* OH MY GOD.

BIRD: I was kidding.

VI: *(That's not the issue. Holds up container.)* You let them get cold!

BIRD: I did? Me personally?

PILAR: If it's such a crisis, you know how to use a microwave.

VI: *(Heads off with the pancakes, doing a snotty impression of her mom.)* "If it's such a crisis, you know how to use a microwave."

(Exits.)

BIRD: Friggin' prom!

PILAR: "I'm gonna end him?"

(They both laugh. An idea hits him.)

BIRD: Hey. Move over here.

PILAR: What?

BIRD: Sit with me.

PILAR: All right…but that's Vi's spot.

BIRD: I think we've established things can change. *(She settles in. He breathes out.)* That's better.

PILAR: Yeah. It is. *(They look at each other: real eye contact. Grinning, almost shy.)* I remember you.

BIRD: *(Feeling the moment.)* I remember you. *(Beat.)*

PILAR: *(Aiming for confidence.)* We got this.

BIRD: *(Hopeful-doubtful.)* Ya think?

PILAR: *(She look at the side where VI exited. Then back at BIRD, hesitating. Surety is hard to hold onto. Wry.)* For now?

(They both laugh gently. And then lean in for a tender kiss. They rest their heads together just as VI returns with the scallion pancakes.)

(VI stops in her tracks when she sees her parents caught in the spell of a moment that is just for them. And, for once, she lets them have it. She beams.)

End of play.

BAD PANDA by Megan Gogerty

Synopsis: They're the last two pandas on earth. It's mating season. One of them falls in love with a crocodile. Who is gay. And then the baby comes. In this sweet celebration of non-traditional families, Gwo Gwo the panda must balance his newfound desire for Chester the crocodile with his obligations to his prescribed panda mate, Marion. The animals eat, mate, splash around in identity politics, wrestle with the ambivalence of parenthood, and love one another as only families can.

Cast Size: 2 Males, 1 Female

CHAOS
THEORY
a   seeking
play
order

BY COURTNEY MEAKER

<u>CHAOS THEORY</u> by Courtney Meaker

Synopsis: When her lover disappears Frannie sinks into a pajamas-only depression. Her friends try to distract her with a book about chaos theory little knowing they're headed down a slippery path through enticing alternate realities. Does the Machine they're building actually work, or are they luring each other into collective delusions of wish-fulfillment? And what if these seductive changes bring about the end of the world?

Cast Size: Diverse Cast of 4

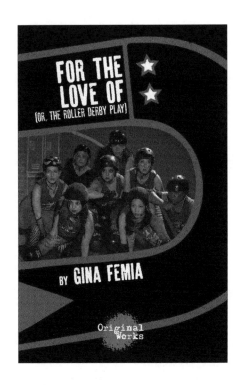

FOR THE LOVE OF (Or, The Roller Derby Play)
by Gina Femia

Synopsis: When Joy gets on the Brooklyn Scallywags and meets the star, Lizzie Lightning, she and her long term partner Michelle find their lives turned upside down. For The Love Of asks how much you're willing to sacrifice – or lose – in order to follow your heart.

Cast Size: 9 Diverse Females

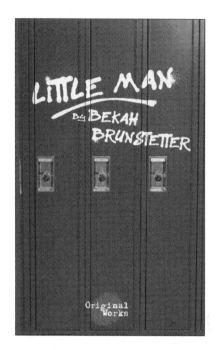

LITTLE MAN by Bekah Brunstetter
Synopsis: Howie has spent the last decade trying to forget
the traumas of high school. But when an invitation to his
ten year reunion arrives, he hops on a plane home to dis-
cover just what happened to the jocks, the prom queens,
and the social outcasts- and whether anyone cares that he's
a millionaire now. With wry wit and penetrating insight,
Bekah Brunstetter's heartbreaking comedy takes us on a
hilariously awkward and unexpectedly moving journey in
which no one can completely abandon who they used to
be.
Cast Size: 3 Males, 3 Females

RULES FOR COMING OUT WHEN YOU'RE IN THE DRIVER'S SEAT OF YOUR MOM'S CAMRY

by Jessica Marie Fisher

Synopsis: "Rules For Coming Out..." is the coming out story for people who are tired of unnecessarily dramatic and unrealistic coming out stories. Almost nobody "KNOWS" completely what their sexuality is – most people have to find the answers through trial and error. Lauren and Liam navigate love, sex, family, identity, relationship abuse and the sticky in-between of queer adolescence, while working through their own imperfect friendship.

Cast Size: 1 Female, 1 Male

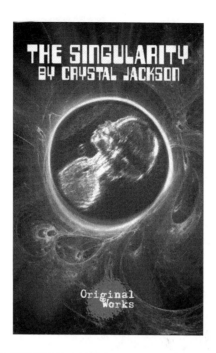

THE SINGULARITY by Crystal Jackson

Synopsis: Astrid, a single lesbian of a certain age, put off motherhood until the absolute last second. Now on her final egg, she has less than 48 hours to acquire the other vital ingredient for conception. Thanks to an awkward young scientist, she gets her hands on a small container of dark matter, a fundamental building block of the universe. With the clock running out and no options left, she decides to improvise with a turkey baster full of the stuff. And it works. Quickly. In just a couple of weeks, she's expanded to three times her normal size. Her baby is coming early, and its arrival has implications for us all.

Cast Size: 5 Males, 1 Female, 1 Trans Female. (Racially diverse)

R & J & Z by Melody Bates

Synopsis: What if Romeo and Juliet got a second chance? "R & J & Z" begins with Act V of Shakespeare's Romeo and Juliet and keeps going, as the famous lovers navigate a world in which death isn't necessarily the end. Set against the historical backdrop of Verona's plague, Melody Bates' new verse play throws old and new characters together over the course of an apocalyptic and action-packed 24 hours. Equally inspired by Shakespeare and modern zombie films, "R & J & Z" pushes the boundaries of theatrical humor and horror.

Cast Size: Diverse Cast of 15-19

NOTES

NOTES

NOTES

Made in the USA
Columbia, SC
20 June 2023